Brown

by Iain Gray

G000068026

Lang**Syne**

PUBLISHING

WRITING *to* REMEMBER

Lang**Syne**

PUBLISHING

WRITING *to* REMEMBER

79 Main Street, Newtongrange,
Midlothian EH22 4NA
Tel: 0131 344 0414   Fax: 0845 075 6085
E-mail: info@lang-syne.co.uk
www.langsyneshop.co.uk

Design by Dorothy Meikle
Printed by Printwell Ltd
© Lang Syne Publishers Ltd 2022

ISBN 978-1-85217-582-5

Brown

MOTTO:
Let majesty flourish.

CREST:
A lion holding a gold
fleur de lis in its paws.

NAME variations include:
Bron
Browne
Broun
Broune

Chapter one:

The origins of popular surnames

by George Forbes and Iain Gray

If you don't know where you came from, you won't know where you're going is a frequently quoted observation and one that has a particular resonance today when there has been a marked upsurge in interest in genealogy, with increasing numbers of people curious to trace their family roots.

Main sources for genealogical research include census returns and official records of births, marriages and deaths – and the key to unlocking the detail they contain is obviously a family surname, one that has been 'inherited' and passed from generation to generation.

No matter our station in life, we all have a surname – but it was not until about the middle of the fourteenth century that the practice of being identified by a particular surname became commonly established throughout the British Isles.

Previous to this, it was normal for a person to be identified through the use of only a forename.

But as population gradually increased and there were many more people with the same forename, surnames were adopted to distinguish one person, or community, from another.

Many common English surnames are patronymic in origin, meaning they stem from the forename of one's father – with 'Johnson,' for example, indicating 'son of John.'

It was the Normans, in the wake of their eleventh century conquest of Anglo-Saxon England, a pivotal moment in the nation's history, who first brought surnames into usage – although it was a gradual process.

For the Normans, these were names initially based on the title of their estates, local villages and chateaux in France to distinguish and identify these landholdings.

Such grand descriptions also helped enhance the prestige of these warlords and generally glorify their lofty positions high above the humble serfs slaving away below in the pecking order who had only single names, often with Biblical connotations as in Pierre and Jacques.

The only descriptive distinctions among the peasantry concerned their occupations, like 'Pierre the swineherd' or 'Jacques the ferryman.'

Roots of surnames that came into usage in England not only included Norman-French, but also Old French, Old Norse, Old English, Middle English, German, Latin, Greek, Hebrew and the Gaelic languages of the Celts.

The Normans themselves were originally Vikings, or 'Northmen', who raided, colonised and eventually settled down around the French coastline.

They had sailed up the Seine in their long-boats in 900AD under their ferocious leader Rollo and ruled the roost in north eastern France before sailing over to conquer England in 1066 under Duke William of Normandy – better known to posterity as William the Conqueror, or King William I of England.

Granted lands in the newly-conquered England, some of their descendants later acquired territories in Wales, Scotland and Ireland – taking not only their own surnames, but also the practice of adopting a surname, with them.

But it was in England where Norman rule and custom first impacted, particularly in relation to the adoption of surnames.

This is reflected in the famous *Domesday Book*, a massive survey of much of England and Wales, ordered by William I, to determine who owned what, what it was worth and therefore how much they were liable to pay in taxes to the voracious Royal Exchequer.

Completed in 1086 and now held in the National Archives in Kew, London, 'Domesday' was an Old English word meaning 'Day of Judgement.'

This was because, in the words of one contemporary chronicler, "its decisions, like those of the Last Judgement, are unalterable."

It had been a requirement of all those English landholders – from the richest to the poorest – that they identify themselves for the purposes of the survey and for future reference by means of a surname.

This is why the *Domesday Book*, although written in Latin as was the practice for several centuries with both civic and ecclesiastical records, is an invaluable source for the early appearance of a wide range of English surnames.

Several of these names were coined in connection with occupations.

These include Baker and Smith, while Cooks, Chamberlains, Constables and Porters were to be found carrying out duties in large medieval households.

The church's influence can be found in names such as Bishop, Friar and Monk while the popular name of Bennett derives from the late fifth to mid-sixth century Saint Benedict, founder of the Benedictine order of monks.

The early medical profession is represented by Barber, while businessmen produced names that include Merchant and Sellers.

Down at the village watermill, the names that cropped up included Millar/Miller, Walker and Fuller, while other self-explanatory trades included Cooper, Tailor, Mason and Wright.

Even the scenery was utilised as in Moor, Hill, Wood and Forrest – while the hunt and the chase supplied names that include Hunter, Falconer, Fowler and Fox.

Colours are also a source of popular surnames, as in Black, Brown, Gray/Grey, Green and White, and would have denoted the colour of the clothing the person habitually wore or, apart from the obvious exception of 'Green', one's hair colouring or even complexion.

The surname Red developed into Reid, while

Blue was rare and no-one wanted to be associated with yellow.

Rather self-important individuals took surnames that include Goodman and Wiseman, while physical attributes crept into surnames such as Small and Little.

Many families proudly boast the heraldic device known as a Coat of Arms, as featured on our front cover.

The central motif of the Coat of Arms would originally have been what was borne on the shield of a warrior to distinguish himself from others on the battlefield.

Not featured on the Coat of Arms, but high-lighted on page three, is the family motto and related crest – with the latter frequently different from the central motif.

Adding further variety to the rich cultural heritage that is represented by surnames is the appearance in recent times in lists of the 100 most common names found in England of ones that include Khan, Patel and Singh – names that have proud roots in the vast sub-continent of India.

Echoes of a far distant past can still be found in our surnames and they can be borne with pride in commemoration of our forebears.

Chapter two:

Battle honours

**Originally a descriptive term for the colour of a
person's hair, complexion, or clothing, Brown is
now one of the most common surnames in
England, but there is nothing commonplace about
the lives, times and achievements of those who
have borne the name down through the centuries
until the present day.**

Variations of 'Brown' exist in every
European language. In France it is le Brun, and in
Germany Brun, or Braun, while other versions are
Bron, Browne, Browyn, Brwne, Brune, Brouin,
Broune, and Broun.

The name le Brune – 'the Brown' – was first
found in present-day Northumberland, only a few
decades after the Norman Conquest of England
in 1066, at a time when much of this vast area
of the north of England was part of the Scottish
kingdom.

A family of le Brune, or Brown, are thought
to have been among those Norman warriors, their
families and retainers who settled in England and later

in Scotland following the conquest – and the surname subsequently grew in popularity.

By the very nature of their geographical location in the north of England, many bearers of the name would have become victims of the interminable and bloody warfare that raged for centuries between the two nations – in common with their namesakes across the border.

In later centuries and on much different fields of battle, many of the name have gained distinction on the field of battle – with two being recipients of the Victoria Cross (VC), the highest award for valour in the face of enemy action for British and Commonwealth forces.

Born in 1898 in Gananoque, Ontario, Harry W. Brown was a Canadian recipient of the honour during the carnage of the First World War.

He had been serving on the Western Front with the 10th Battalion, Canadian Expeditionary Force when, during the battle of Hill 70 in August of 1917, he braved heavy enemy fire to take an important message back from the front line to his support lines – thereby saving the lives of a number of his comrades.

Wounded in the action, he died the following

day, while his VC is now on display at the Canadian War Museum, Ottawa.

Walter Brown, born in 1885 in New Norfolk, Tasmania, was an Australian recipient of the VC during the First World War.

It was while serving in the infantry with the Australian Army's 20th Battalion that, in July of 1918 at Villers-Bretonneux, he single-handedly destroyed a German machine-gun post and took a number of prisoners.

Returning to civilian life at the end of the conflict, on the outbreak of the Second World War and aged 54, he lied about not only his age but also his background in order to re-enlist in the army.

It was while serving with the Royal Australian Artillery that he was killed in action in Singapore in February of 1942 following the Japanese attack on Malaya; his VC is now on display at the Australian War Museum, Canberra.

In the skies above the Western Front during the First World War, Captain Arthur Roy Brown was the Canadian flying ace officially credited by the RAF with having shot down the famous German ace Manfred von Richthofen, more colourfully known as the Red Baron.

Born in 1893 and enlisting with the Royal Flying Corps (RFC) – later known as the Royal Air Force (RAF) following the amalgamation in April of 1918 of the RFC and the Royal Naval Air Squadron (RNAS) – his first 'kill' came in July of 1917 when he shot down a German Albatross D. III.

Three unconfirmed and two unconfirmed kills followed, but it was on April 21, 1918, that he was engaged in the aerial action for which he became particularly famous.

This was when, involved with other pilots of his squadron in a fast and furious dogfight with fighters of *Jagdstaffel II*, led by the Red Baron, he apparently shot him down.

But while the RAF officially credited Brown with the death of the Red Baron, it now appears more likely that the German ace, who had been forced to descend to an extremely low altitude as Brown attacked him, was actually shot down from ground level by Australian Army machine-gunners.

Brown later donated the seat of the Fokker triplane the Red Baron had been flying to the Royal Canadian Military Institute.

He died in 1944, while he is portrayed by the

actor Don Stroud in the 1971 film *Von Richthofen and Brown*.

Another noted aviator was Sir Arthur Whitten Brown, born to American parents in 1886 in Glasgow, where his father had been investigating the prospect of setting up a factory in Clydebank.

Following a distinguished flying career during the First World War and also being captured after being shot down, it was in June of 1919 that, as navigator, and with John Alcock as pilot, he made the first successful non-stop transatlantic flight.

This was in a modified Vickers Vimy bomber that flew 1,980 miles (3,168km) from St John's, Newfoundland, to Clifden, Connemara, in Ireland.

Knighted along with Alcock in recognition of the pioneering feat, he died in 1948.

Chapter three:

Loyal service

From servants of royalty to servants of the people, other bearers of the Brown name have made their mark on the historical record.

It was shortly after Queen Victoria and her consort Prince Albert had Balmoral Castle in Aberdeenshire built as their Scottish retreat, that a colourful and charismatic character known as John Brown came to work there from nearby Crathie as a gamekeeper and general estate worker.

He rapidly gained royal favour, becoming Prince Albert's personal ghillie and, following the consort's death in 1861, the personal servant of the Queen herself.

Victoria was bereft over the loss of her beloved Albert, and Brown appears to have provided much needed comfort and solace throughout her long years of mourning.

The blunt speaking farmer's son, born in Crathie in 1826, was despised by the Queen's immediate family, royal courtiers and other servants who resented and were jealous of the favours the monarch granted him and the easy informality he was allowed to adopt towards her.

Among the many gifts he received from a grateful Victoria were two medals especially created for him, the Faithful Servant Medal and the Devoted Service Medal, while she also commissioned a portrait of her loyal ghillie.

He died at Windsor Castle in 1883, after contracting a chill that could have been averted had he immediately taken to his sickbed. Brown was buried in his native Crathie.

Victoria was inconsolable with grief at the loss of her loyal retainer and had a life-sized statue of him erected in the grounds of Balmoral.

Following her death in 1901, however, the statue was removed to a less prominent spot, while Edward VII set about destroying all other reminders of Brown that he could find.

Speculation was rife during Brown and Victoria's lifetimes as to the exact nature of their close relationship, with whispered rumours that it was of a sexual nature.

The speculation continues to the present day, and was recently refuelled with the discovery of diaries that make the startling claim that the Reverend

Norman MacLeod, Victoria's chaplain, had made a deathbed confession that he had reluctantly presided over the secret marriage of the Queen to her humble servant.

Doubt has been cast on the veracity of the account committed to the diaries, however, but doubtless the speculation will continue for many more years to come.

Across thousands of miles of ocean from the farm in Crathie where John Brown was born, another John Brown, born in Torrington, Connecticut, in 1800, is revered as the American abolitionist whose militant opposition to slavery lit the spark of the Civil War that eventually freed the slaves.

He had a number of nicknames, including Oswatomie Brown, Old Man Brown, and Captain Brown, and it was as a military leader that he led a raid on the federal armoury at Harpers Ferry, in present day West Virginia, in 1859.

He was captured and hanged, but his memory survives in the song *John Brown's Body*, which became a favourite marching song of the Union troops during the American Civil War of 1861-65.

In contemporary British politics, James Gordon Brown, better known as Gordon Brown, is the British Labour Party politician who served as Prime Minister from 2007 until 2010.

Previous to this, under Prime Minister Tony Blair, he served from 1997 to 2007 as Chancellor of the Exchequer – making him to date the longest serving holder of the office in modern history.

Born in 1951 and the son of a Church of Scotland minister who had a profound influence on his own social and moral outlook, he was raised along with his older brother John and younger brother Andrew in his father's manse in Kirkcaldy, Fife.

An academic prodigy, he was aged only 16 when accepted to study history at Edinburgh University. He graduated with a first class degree, while he later also gained a PhD in the subject.

Meanwhile, it had been while playing rugby at his local school that he sustained an injury that left him blind in his left eye, while he later successfully underwent surgery to save his right eye.

His first foray into the political world had been when he served, as a student, as Rector of Edinburgh University.

After a career that included lecturing in politics

and working for a time as a television journalist, in 1983 he was elected Labour MP for Dunfermline East and, later, what is now the constituency of Kirkcaldy and Cowdenbeath.

It was after the resignation of Tony Blair as Labour leader and Prime Minister in 2007 that Brown was selected to replace him in both posts – holding them until Labour's defeat at the 2010 General Election.

Married in 2000 to Sarah Macaulay, he is the father of two sons – while the couple's first child died only a few days after her birth.

Named in 2009 by the Appeal of Conscience Foundation as World Statesman of the Year and in 2012 appointed a United Nations Special Envoy on Global Education, he is also the author of noted works that include his 1986 *Maxton: A Biography* and his 2010 *Beyond the Crash: Overcoming the First Crisis of Globalisation*.

After lending his considerable and impassioned political weight for a "No" vote in the referendum for Scottish Independence in September of 2014, he announced three months later his retiral from active Parliamentary politics.

One particularly colourful senior Labour

Party politician was George Brown, born in 1914 in Lambeth, near London.

From a working class background, he rose through the ranks of the Labour Party to serve for a time as its deputy leader and, under Prime Minister Harold Wilson, as Foreign Secretary from 1966 to 1968.

Probably through the pressures of the high offices he held, however, he had an unfortunate relationship with alcohol, and was involved in a number of embarrassing drink-fuelled incidents.

Retiring from government in March of 1968, he was later ennobled as Lord George-Brown of Jevington in the County of Sussex; he died in 1985.

Born in 1881 in Torquay, Devon, Alfred Brown was a senior British Liberal Party politician.

Serving during the First World War in the Somerset Light Infantry, he was awarded the Military Cross (MC), and first entered Parliament in 1923.

In the National Government of Labour's leader Ramsay MacDonald, he served in 1931 as Parliamentary Secretary to the Ministry of Health, while in 1935 he was appointed Minister of Labour.

He was renowned for not only the extremely fast delivery of his speeches in the House of Commons, but also for the loudness of his voice.

So strong was his voice that on one occasion fellow politician Stanley Baldwin was startled to hear it booming out in No. 11 Downing Street. When informed that it was merely Brown 'speaking to Scotland', Baldwin famously asked: "Why doesn't he use the telephone?" he died in 1962.

Browns have also stamped their mark on the historical record through pioneering work in the sciences.

Born Herbert Brovarnik in London in 1912, the son of Ukrainian-Jewish immigrants to Britain and later changing his surname, Herbert Brown was the chemist who, along with his colleague Georg Wittig, won the 1979 Nobel Prize for Chemistry for their work on the compounds of boron and hydrogen known as boranes.

Holder of a number of positions that included professor of inorganic chemistry at Purloe University, Indiana, he died in 2004.

Born in Edinburgh in 1838, Alexander Crum Brown was the Scottish organic chemist who discovered the carbon double bond of ethylene – contributing greatly to the development of the modern plastics industry.

Holder of a number of important academic

posts including professor of chemistry at Edinburgh University from 1869 to 1908, he died in 1922.

One particularly feisty bearer of the proud name of Brown was the socialite and philanthropist Margaret "Molly" Brown, née Tobin, the survivor of the 1912 sinking of the *Titanic* who became better known as The Unsinkable Molly Brown.

Born in 1867 in Hannibal, Missouri, she married the wealthy mining engineering entrepreneur James Brown, but the couple separated in 1909 after 23 years of marriage.

As a first class passenger aboard the *Titanic* on its maiden voyage to New York, after disaster struck she not only helped fellow passengers into lifeboats but also plied an oar herself and insisted that the crewman in charge of her lifeboat – Lifeboat No. 6 – return closer to the stricken vessel to attempt to pick up more survivors.

She died in 1932, while a Broadway musical based on her life and times, *The Unsinkable Molly Brown*, was produced in 1961 and adapted for a film of the same name in 1964.

Chapter four:

On the world stage

Born in 1921, Robert Brown was the English actor best known for his role of 'M' in a number of James Bond films.

It was following the death of the actor Bernard Lee, who had played the role of Bond's secret intelligence chief 'M' that Brown made his first appearance in the role in the 1983 *Octopussy*.

Previous to this, he had appeared in the 1977 Bond film *The Spy Who Loved Me*, in the role of Admiral Hargreaves.

With other film credits that include the 1966 *One Million Years B.C.* and television credits that include the 1950s' *Ivanhoe* series, he died in 2003.

Born in 1952, William Gerard Brown was the Australian actor and playwright better known as **Bille Brown**. Beginning his career in the early 1990s with the Queensland Theatre Company, he went on to play with the Royal Shakespeare Company and later on the Broadway stage, while film credits include the 1997 *Fierce Creatures*, sequel to the 1988 *A Fish Called Wanda*.

He died in 2013, two years after having been appointed a Member of the Order of Australia.

Best known for his role from 1954 to 1959 of Lieutenant Ripley "Rip" Masters in the television series *The Adventures of Rin Tin Tin*, **James E. Brown** was the American actor born in 1920 near Abilene, Texas.

A tennis player before taking up acting as a career, his big screen credits include the 1942 *Wake Island*, the 1949 *Sands of Iwo Jima* and the 1961 *When the Clock Strikes*; he died in 1992.

Born in 1891 in Holgate, Ohio, Joseph Evans Brown was the American author and comedian better known as **Joe E. Brown**.

He died in 1973, with film credits that include the 1935 *A Midsummer Night's Dream* and the 1959 *Some Like it Hot*, in which he played the role of Osgood Fielding III.

Behind the camera lens, **Bruce Brown**, born in San Francisco in 1937, is the documentary film director recognised as a pioneer in the genre known as surfing films.

These include his 1958 *Slippery When Wet*, the 1959 *Surf Crazy* and, from 1964, *The Endless Summer*.

His son, **Dana Brown**, born in 1959, has followed in his father's footsteps by producing films that include his 2003 *Step Into Liquid* and the 2009 *Highwater*.

Known for his collaboration with fellow American film producer Richard D. Zanuck, son of producer Darryl F. Zanuck, **David Brown** was born in New York City in 1916.

With credits that include the 1973 *The Sting*, the 1975 *Jaws*, the 1982 *The Verdict*, the 1989 *Driving Miss Daisy* and the 2000 *Chocolat*, he died in 2010, while along with his collaborator Zanuck he was the recipient in 1990 of the Irving G. Thalberg Memorial Award from the Academy of Motion Picture Arts and Sciences.

Bearers of the Brown name have also excelled in the highly competitive world of sport.

Born in Bengal, India in 1915, **Arthur Brown** was the British athlete who won a gold medal at the 1936 Olympics in Munich in the 4x400-metres relay event.

Also winner of the British Amateur Athletics Association (AAA) championships in the 400-metres event in 1936 and 1938 and in the 800-metres event in 1939, he died in 1995.

On the fields of European football, **Scott Brown**, born in 1985, is the Scottish central midfielder who was appointed captain of Celtic in 2010.

First capped for his national team in 2005, his home village is Hill O' Beath, in Fife, where the late Rangers and Scotland international legend Jim Baxter also grew up.

Born in 1926 in Kennoway, Fife, **Allan Brown** was the Scotland internationalist and manager who played for teams that include East Fife, Blackpool, Luton Town, Portsmouth and Wigan Athletic.

He died in 2011, while teams he managed include Torquay United and Nottingham Forest.

On the cricket pitch, **David Brown**, born in 1942 in Walsall, Staffordshire is the English former cricketer who between 1965 and 1969 represented his nation in 26 Test matches.

Bearers of the Brown name have also stamped a distinctive mark on the landscape, most notably Lancelot Brown, better known as **Capability Brown**.

Born in 1716 in the small village of Kirkharle, Northumberland, he rose from apprentice gardener at Sir William Loraine's estate at Kirkharle Hall to become recognised as 'England's greatest gardener.'

Moving to Buckinghamshire in 1741, he served on the gardening staff on Lord Cobham's estate at Stowe, working under William Kent, a pioneer of the 'English style' of landscape gardening.

Refining Kent's techniques, he became a much sought after landscape architect and gardener, responsible for the design of more than 170 gardens for country estates throughout Britain.

These include Addenbury House, Oxfordshire, Alnwick Castle, in his native Northumberland, Battle Abbey, East Sussex and Bowood House in Wiltshire.

He died in 1783, while his nickname of Capability Brown arose from his 'sales pitch' to potential clients that their estates had great 'capability' for improvement.

In the creative world of the written word, **Dan Brown** is the internationally best-selling American author born in 1964 in Exeter, New Hampshire.

The son of a mathematics teacher and author, he developed an interest from an early age in mathematical puzzles, codes, ciphers and symbols – an interest that is reflected in his conspiracy theory-based novels.

These include his 2003 *The Da Vinci Code*, adapted for film in 2006, and *Angels and Demons*, adapted for film in 2009, while other best-sellers include his 2009 *The Lost Symbol* and, from 2013, *Inferno*.

A best-seller in the 'techno-thriller' genre of fiction, **Dale Brown** was born in 1956 in Buffalo, New York.

A former navigator-bombardier with the United States Air Force and the recipient of a number of military honours that include the Air Force Commendation Medal, his many novels include his 1987 *Flight of the Old Dog*, the 1998 *The Tinman* and, from 1999, *Battle Born*.

Born in 1869 in Ochiltree, East Ayrshire, **George Douglas Brown** was the Scottish novelist whose best known work is his 1901 *The House with the Green Shutters*.

Published under the name of 'George Douglas' and of the genre known as realist fiction, it centres around characters in the fictional town of Barbie – based on his home village of Ochiltree.

He died only a year after publication of the novel, while The Green Shutters Festival of Working Class Writing is held annually in the village in his honour and the house in which he was born is now The Green Shutters Pub.

Another noted Scottish writer was the poet and novelist **George Mackay Brown**, born in 1921 in Stromness, in the Orkney Islands.

It was from Stromness that he penned a number of acclaimed works that include the novels *Vinland* and *Beside the Ocean of Time*, winner of the 1994 Scottish Saltire Book of the Year Award and which was also listed for the Booker Prize for Fiction.

The recipient of an OBE and with poems that include *Hamnavoe*, he died in 1996, while a plaque to him was unveiled in 2005 in the Writers' Museum in the Royal Mile, Edinburgh.

One truly remarkable bearer of the name was the Irish writer and painter **Christy Brown**, born in Dublin in 1932.

Afflicted since birth with severe cerebral palsy, with the help and encouragement of his family and others he nevertheless learned to write and draw using the toes of his left foot.

His immense struggle with everyday life is poignantly detailed in his best-selling autobiography *My Left Foot*, adapted for a film of the same title in 1989.

The actor Daniel Day-Lewis won an Academy Award for his portrayal of Brown, while

Brenda Fricker also won an award for her portrayal of his mother.

He died in 1981, while other highly acclaimed works include his 1970 *Down All the Days* and poetry collections that include *Come Softly to My Wake* and *Of Snails and Skylarks*.

From literature to art, **Ford Madox Brown** was the English painter who specialised in themes of social history.

Born in Calais in 1821, the son of a naval purser, he studied art in Antwerp and later became associated with the artistic set known as the Pre-Raphaelites, although he was never an actual member of this group that included his friend Dante Gabriel Rossetti.

He died in 1893, while his most famous works include his *The Last of England* and *Work*, that depicts 'navvies', or labourers, digging up a road in London.

In a different artistic genre, **Martin Brown**, born in Melbourne in 1959, is the Australian cartoonist and illustrator best known as the main illustrator of the popular *Horrible Histories* series of books.

From art to the world of music, **Joe Brown**, born in 1941 in Swarby, Lincolnshire, is the English entertainer who, in addition to a successful stage, film and television career, enjoyed success as a singer in the 1960s with hits that include *The Darktown Strutters Ball*, *A Picture of You* and *That's What Love Will Do*.

The recipient of an MBE for his services to entertainment, he starred between 1965 and 1968 in the West End musical *Charlie Girl* and the 1965 musical comedy film *Three Hats for Lisa*.

An inductee of the Rock and Roll Hall of Fame, **James Brown** was the American recording artist and musician recognised as 'The Godfather of Soul' and one of the founding fathers of the funk music genre.

Born in 1933 in Barnwell, South Carolina, he enjoyed hit singles that include *Papa's Got a Brand New Bag*, *It's a Man's Man's World* and his 1968 *Say it Loud – I'm Black and I'm Proud*; ranked seventh in *Rolling Stone* magazine's list of its 100 greatest artists of all time, he died in 2006.

In a different musical genre, **Ian Brown**, born in Warrington in 1963, is the lead singer of the English alternative rock band The Stone Roses.

Born in 1942, **Arthur Brown** is the English rock musician known for his flamboyant stage act and the hit single *Fire*, taken from his 1968 debut album *The Crazy World of Arthur Brown*.

In the challenging world of business, **Sir David Brown**, born in 1904 and who died in 1993, was the English entrepreneur known for his ownership from 1947 until the 1970s of Aston Martin.

It was during his period of ownership of the upmarket car company that it manufactured the 'DB' series of Aston Martins – with 'DB' his initials and the DB5 the car famously driven by the character James Bond in a number of the Bond series of films.

One bearer of the Brown name with a rather unusual claim to fame is Englishwoman Louise Brown, who on July 25, 1978 became the first human to be born after conception by in vitro fertilisation (IVF).

She was born in Oldham General Hospital, in Greater Manchester, while the successful IVF technique had been developed by Patrick Steptoe and Robert Edwards.

Four years later, her sister Natalie was also conceived by IVF – making her the world's 40th IVF baby.